THE LOVE DYNASTY

A series on true stories of Love, pain, betrayal and victory

Book One

Phanie Neri

Author's note

Hello Reader,

I am Phanie Neri; the author you are just going to fall in love with. I grew up knowing I wanted to be a writer.

However, I was confident I wanted to write exciting fictitious works until I started experiencing genuine life experiences in my love life. We all know how events create our perspectives towards life and sculpt us into having diverse outlooks. It was not different for me. My encounters created a completely new notion for me. I found myself transitioning from wishing to be a fictitious writer, who gives non-existent characters life, to being a writer who presents people's lives the way it is; presenting tales of love, self discovery and the hardships individuals have experienced. I adore delivering intriguing tales and I plan to retain my grasp on my readers with true stories from beautiful people all around the world. The most lovely part about these tales is they come directly from the sources whose life it reflects. I do respect individuals and have received their consent to relate their story. It is such an honour for me to accomplish this. I believe it takes a huge amount of bravery for anybody to speak their tale, particularly when it reveals their shortcomings and fragility.

So, I encourage you, when you read these tales with keen attention, recognize that life really is not predictable and in the arena of Love, everything is conceivable. Love tales are not always beautiful but every love story is motivating and worth discussing since it always helps us obtain a whole new perspective.

Enjoy keeping devoted to my book series and one day I hope we get to hear your tale too.

Yours,

Phanie Neri

Dedication

To everyone that still has the courage to believe in Love even if lovers once failed them.
And to those who have doubts about true love, just believe, it will come along.

Table of contents

Chapter One

Unbreakable

Love attacked me in the most improbable manner...

Like every other individual, I had my dreams. I knew everything I wanted for myself and most significantly, what I didn't want. I put forth the required efforts to be the best version of myself. However, life constantly occurs and its eventualities frequently arrive unexpectedly.

Same was the situation with me.

After putting all my efforts, I found myself following on routes that were weird; utterly off of my chosen direction. I was caught in unwelcome circles and had terrible repercussions. By the time I glanced back, I had gone so far into filth, stuck in a hole with no escape strategy.

But you know the amazing thing about God, he is an excellent HERO! He shows you the light even amid your deep darkness. So, after approximately six years or so of squandering my life, and surviving heartbreaks here and there, the beam of light reached me and I submitted entirely.

What was the light? A Man! A lovely, kind, loving guy. An in-depthly attractive man with the most unique logic. The weird thing was, I saw him weeks before he showed up there, in a dream. I needed release from my sorrows and the heartache that nearly broke me and the ghosts from my dreadful past blunders; I simply wanted rescue and Benedict's presence made it happen.

I had returned to school, to clear up whatever was keeping me from graduating. One evening, on my way to fetch supper, I was stopped by him. Physically, he did not look like what I dreamed of, but my Spirit immediately knew. He appeared uncomfortable and not that cute but these things are often contextual, what counts is what your Spirit says.

So, I followed his example. Truthfully, our connection was not what I anticipated. I had assumed perfection was when we had a specific degree of accuracy in our manner of operation; or when we followed a certain system.

For instance, every one supports your choice of a partner, sees only the positive in him and likes having him around or you continue things the way it has been followed from the beginning. In that scenario, if a connection isn't in this shape, then it is all incorrect.

CLICHÉ!

Had I not had an initial conviction, I would have given up on us since all the circumstances were incorrect; harmful energy from my parents, Aunties and uncles. There was also my Ugly past and its traits banging continuously on our new existence.

At some time, it appeared as if 'WE' would be history and forgotten.

Benedict's patience and consistency with these things is pretty impressive. He stood through the blaze like a rock and never pondered a break up for one day. My parent's Negativity towards us did not even push him one inch. He thought we were destined to be and it was just a matter of time.

Most times, I was even the one that jittered a lot. I had innumerable anxieties particularly everytime I recalled my irresponsible past. I believed he may simply

walk on and be with anybody else. We had a
kid, another and a third while still waiting
for father to understand how suited we were
for one another, since he was not prepared
to pay bride price or even present my fiancé
to my kinsmen because I am African and
this is our custom.

I and Benedict proceeded on to complete a
legal joining and began living as man and
wife. Months after the third kid, Daddy let
his high barriers break and asked for us to
come.

He accepted Benedict and blessed our
Union. My queries were: what took you so
long Daddy?

Now, he wants me to forget the days I was
left in abandonment because I brought
'shame' to him? The days he wanted me to
leave my children with Ben and come back
home to get my life fixed?

The fact that for a period of 6 months or so, daddy did not talk to me? The most distressing is the fact that he was not able to create a good connection with his grandkids before departing this world. Depressing.

Well, happily, he at least met them and spent some time with them . It saddens me that he is gone now. However, I take delight in the fact that he finally gave us his blessings. That means so much to me. I am delighted that I discovered light at my darkest moment and this light has lingered for a long time and the hurts of the past seem so distant today.

Only love can truly heal the wounds of the past.

...That is what Love can do! We are counting down to FOREVER, me and my Lover turned Partner for life.

SARAH.

Chapter Two

$\mathcal{A}$ Smile From an Angel

A mother's love is a force ; a force that shields her beloved.

At the beginning of my life, I was pure and innocent.

 My mother frequently told me stories of how she loves to see me grin as my smiles offcred so much pleasure to her. Those smiles must have been so significant to her that she searched fervently for them.
I was believed to be pleasant and kind hearted and this prompted my parcnts to shower me with so much attention. We dwelt in a modest town in the southern portion of my country. My parents did not

have everything but they were happy and so in love that it did not matter if we were broke periodically. I was surrounded by people who loved me and my smile never left my lips because my life was amazing!

Until sometime ago, things became terrible. My parents turned from lovebirds to bitter adversaries. There were countless issues between them. So much hostility grew within their marriage and they suddenly handed me the most heartbreaking news I had heard, they were calling it quits on their love story; as in, their marriage ended. All those years together slid away and the memories were drowned in the sea of contempt that they both now felt for one other. If you have been in-between divorced parents, you would know how awful it may be. I was absolutely depressed, losing touch with myself. I was around 18 when this happened. I lost trust in love, even in God.

I got reclusive and began using toxic depressants to set myself free from the burning sorrow I felt every time I thought of my parents. I switched from being a calm girl to becoming a gigantic catastrophe!

I fell so deep into nastiness that by the time I knew what was happening to me, I had over shot my limitations. I was now an alcoholic, a drug addict, and a whore. The 'whore' element was the scariest! I was not following the trend or following these guys for money, I just did it to uncover some value for myself. But what did I do? I ended up complicating my life even more.

Soon, males knew me as the frail person who had no self worth and would give herself without resistance. For four years, my life stayed in this mess until some time later, I met a young kid, Jaden. Jaden was just different. He picked me up that day from a friend's house party and took me home, to his apartment. Most men would rather take me to a hotel as I was regarded as too worthless to be allowed inside their residences. However, Jade on the contrary, did the exact opposite. He had me take a hot bath and put me in a comfy room to rest my head. It looked odd, but he did it. I waited all night for Jade but he did not show up. It was the weirdest experience I had ever had in my life from a guy; a full fledged man with a fantastic physique, seeing all the delights in my body and not wanting to claim it all. I was not sure how to feel. So I managed to hold myself till dawn. I ended up staying at Jaden's place for four days, without being touched.

We held hands periodically, we chatted about a variety of themes such as God, marriage, sex, visions and dreams. I felt myself calming up. I could feel walls melting oddly.

After my little vacation at Jaden's, I noted some apparent changes in my life. After a while, I began following Jaden to church and sought God more than ever. Sometimes, I slid back to sin a bit and began feeling guilty but Jaden was always there to hold my hands. Two months after meeting Jaden, I WOKE UP ONE MORNING FEELING NAUSEOUS. I WAS PREGNANT! Being pregnant was not really the issue, the trouble was that I felt convinced I could not pinpoint exactly who was responsible. I watched the life I thought I had started to make afresh, falling away before me. I could not keep the baby. I was beginning to explore God. Now, this would put a stop to my life and I was not ready. Also, my mother had passed on to eternity and my father had remarried. I was not sure what to do. After a month passed, I decided to involve Jaden in my problem. When I told him, he sighed and spoke gently with care and precision "It is probably the will of God for you. You may just have to keep it". He insisted I was going to have the baby. He kept telling me that I would find atonement

by having the baby. He urged me to carry on
that he was going to be there by my side
through it all. It took me some while, but I
agreed.

 I went through the first trimester pouting
and distancing from everyone. Jaden stood
by me. By my second trimester, it became
clear that this was true. I began seeking to
connect with my child. I began to feel love
for my foetus and this emotion rose by the
second. I finally realized myself merging
with this child and relying on its slightest
kicks and actions for joy. I found myself
then yearning to see it smile and expecting
to have my heart filled with happiness, as
my mother had said years before about me.
Jaden made sure I followed every
conceivable routine I was meant to follow
along my path and ultimately on my 22nd
birthday, I started feeling contractions. It
was a really exciting occasion because it
symbolized the beginning of a new life for

me. Ten hours later, my baby made his magnificent arrival into the world. I cradled him in my arms and I felt so calm. There was so much peace around me. I clasped his little hands in mine and kissed his forehead and all the sorrows I had been through in all those years seemed to immediately disappear; they were actually gone forever! I named my son Jaden, after Jaden; it just seemed like the right thing to do in honour of a true friend who effortlessly gave me a reason to believe in life, myself and love.

We presently dwell in a different location, having the happiest time of our lives. The bigger Jaden is now married, with children while I am happily a single mum.

Having my son was the best decision I ever made. His smiles undoubtedly provide joy and hope to me and it reminds me of how much God loves me. I am now a better version of myself and a lot more responsible with my life. God did offer redemption to

me through my child. So I know that babies
are essentially blessings from God, no
matter how one chooses to interpret their
arrival.

JANE

Chapter Three

Complicado

Emotional strength is a virtue most people lack. Handle other people's emotions with care because You'll never know who is too weak to bear a wreck.

Life, they say, is a journey through experiences. One cannot claim to pass through life without walking through different streets of experiences; including the good, the bad and the ugly.

These experiences inspire our views and help us to build our personality even better.

This particular experience I want to share happened to me a long time ago and it was a thrilling encounter; one that left an indelible mark on my memory, making it a haunting experience.

I was an undergraduate student, 24 and your typical 'glam boy'; rich and famous.

I was known for my big invention in my Uni days; the first classic Male Salon in that area. I was just the boy with the swag. It was typical for a young handsome man, that popular to be in a relationship. So, I was with a beautiful woman, Annie.

Anita was my everything. I put her first Even before myself. She seemed to bring some kind of completion to me and I could not trade that for anything else in the world. We were just a perfect fit. She loved me deeply and I simply adored her. As a matter of fact, she was my first real girlfriend and after a year with her, I was certain that we were made for each other.

In Spite of how I felt about Anita, I was
certain there was something enigmatic
about her. I often felt like she had some
huge secret I was not aware of. One
beautiful day, I paid her a visit; cos I did
that often, bearing gifts to make her feel the
weight of my love. This particular visit was
to be the genesis of some unfortunate events
of my life.

That day, I went with one of my friends;
Kendy. He had never met the lady he heard
so much about and wanted to meet her to
understand why I felt so entangled to her.
Anita gave us a warm welcome, as she would
always do and stepped out for a bit to pick
up some things from the hostel portal.
Kendy, being a very inquisitive person,
decided to look through her photo album, to
know more about her personality and of
course view her killer looks from other
dimensions.

As we looked through her photo album, we noticed she took countless photos with one particular man who seemed like he was in his mid 50s. I normally would not be bothered with such a thing; I could have given other explanations but Kendy would not have it. He was prepared to swear that Anita must have something romantic going on with the man for her to be in compromising poses with him. He advised me to be wise.

As much as not believing him sounded good and danger free, I damned it and waited for her to return. When she came back, she could feel the change in the environment because I was now feeling disappointed and anger was welling up inside of me. All I needed was some closure on the matter. One part of me wanted to believe my lie but the other part was sold out to Kendy's truth. Immediately I asked her, she broke down in tears and got down to the floor. I was of course confused. She wept so much that she

began shaking. I held her up and tried to
gather as much information regarding the
matter as I could to help me make a
decision. She begged me to stay with her.
She said she would die if I left her. She truly
was courting the man, she was betrothed by
Family to him but she claimed that she had
no feelings whatsoever for him; that if she
ended up with him, she would be the most
unhappy woman on earth.

I really was not sure how to feel or what to
say. But the only thing I could think of was
how to get myself home and call it quits.
After long minutes of speechlessness, I told
Anita to give me space. That was my indirect
way of putting an indefinite hold on our
relationship.

Moving on from someone you deeply adored
is always the most difficult part of life. To
get over her, I tripled my involvement with
school, business and of course other women.

Then came Catherine; young beautiful and voluptuous blonde babe. She had eyes like a goddess. I was not letting her go. We got entangled in the web of lust and eventually Something that seemed like love and our lives set in motion. It was good to be with another woman, but in all honesty, thoughts of Anita had glued to my memory and therefore became indelible. No matter how much I tried to convince myself otherwise, Cathy could never take Annie's place. It was an emotional struggle for me for about three months.

Taking a walk isn't always that easy...

But One day, I broke free!

I made that move towards Annie, putting aside the possible risks involved in going back to her. She was more than willing to have me back, as she had been waiting for me to forgive her and take her back. Falling in love with her again was effortless and we just ignited our lost passion with ease. Soon, our love was aflame once again. Then I knew it was time to part ways with edible Cathy(as she was popularly called).

Every relationship is a gamble because you will never completely know what your partner is capable of doing. Certain behavioural attributes of your partner, when finally unveiled, may cause you to fall into so much shock and be overthrown by disbelief. Just pray the unveiling does not reveal demons, else you are done for. Cathy's unveiling was filled with extremity and rashness. What I beheld?... Was pure evil!

We had ended things, at the rebirth of my relationship with Anita. I explained to her that I could not be without Anita. She sounded hurt but promised she would move on. I was quite impressed with her sense of maturity and understanding. After sometime, she began stalking me with countless phone calls, Calling me all manner of names. I did not want to react because I knew she was going through some kind of psychological trauma caused by our break up.

Besides, I and Anita were waxing strong. So, I had little time for a nagging ex-girlfriend. It seemed as though the more I ignored, the more she upped her game. The next line of action she took was spreading dirty rumors about me deflowering her and leaving her stranded. She knew my personality and how much fame I had obtained in our environment and she was determined to rub me off of that prestige. I was not denying the fact that in our three months of uninteresting relationship, we did get intimate a couple of times but I was sure she was not a virgin. So, I did not understand why she would be cooking up such unsolicited lies.

After the dust had been raised, she made an attempt to see me. She called and asked that I pay her a visit. At first, I did not want to go to her but I felt that she could be wanting to apologise for her behaviour. So, I accepted my self conviction and went to her house. I tried to question her about her lies and she said I broke her heart badly. She began touching me and trying to get me aroused. I resisted her because I did not feel that way about her anymore. All I needed were explanations. She began crying loudly. I begged her to stop. I told her that I was not going to leave Anita because she was my soul mate.

Unbelievable, was her next move. She got up, wiped her eyes and pulled out a plastic bottle that had a liquid content inside of it. I was not sure what she was up to. She lifted the bottle to her mouth and emptied the content into her mouth, swallowing with heavy gulps. Before I knew what was happening, she collapsed on the floor and foam was coming out of the corners of her mouth. It was at that moment that my inner mind reached out to my senses and the implication of what had happened struck me with authenticity. She had tried to commit suicide! She took a mixture of chemicals. I rushed out to call for help.

Emotional strength is a virtue most people lack. Handle other people's emotions with care cos you'll never know.

Everything happened so fast... She was taken to the hospital and I was taken to the police station for questioning. I spent three nights behind bars, waiting for my freedom and justification. I narrated the story over and over, indicating my innocence in the whole matter. Her parents threatened to mess me up, they swore that I would be jailed forever if their daughter died. I was not sure what to do. One thing was, I never allowed the uniformed men to intimidate me, as is their custom. I kept screaming my innocence at every given opportunity.

At some point, one of the police officers, a kind gentleman, advised me to just pray nothing would happen to Cathy, because if her life was tampered with, that I would certainly go in for it and it wouldn't matter that I considered myself innocent. At that moment, my perspective changed and all I could pray for was her good health and life.

Eventually, God came through for me and defended me. She began responding to treatment and when she was stable, she wrote her report; in which she stated that I was not at fault in any way, that she was just so obsessed with me and thought she would not survive without me.

Funny.... So funny. Imagine if Cathy had died, I would have been an inmate by now.

Well, Cathy is alive and well. Anita finally married her betrothed and I am happily married to my Bone! 'The Cathy Saga' as I like to call it, taught me that emotional strength isn't common among all humans, and for that reason, we should look deeply before we drag people into emotional entanglements because they may be too weak to handle disappointments...

ANTHONY.

Chapter 4

T*wisted*

A painful experience would be holding up a rose for your soulmate and seeing that soulmate entangled with another...
A young man once said "Life can throw several balls of challenges at you. But the most challenging of them all are the throws that come from people you hold so dearly because nothing can be as heartbreaking as having people you love and cherish pierce your heart with betrayal."

I am that young man! I have lived with a painful heartbreak that it was only until recently that I began teaching myself to love and live again. They say men should Man up when they hurt, I am so sorry to have disappointed my gender but I simply couldn't get myself to play emotionless especially considering my age at the time.

I am not your regular outgoing guy, I never was. I was withdrawn from the crowd and mostly struggled to fit in. As a matter of fact, I was dealing with my esteem when Zara found me. It was sometime in the mid-era of the first decade of 2000's and we were both in Secondary school. Zara was the direct opposite of all that I was. She was bold, full of courage and very expressive. It cost her nothing to say things exactly how she felt it. I was singing that day, somewhere close to the female dormitory and Zara heard my voice. She was with some of her friends and she walked up to me, without a single shame and said "You sing so beautifully, like a woman. Could we be a singing duo"?
We were teenagers remember and in our era, youngsters were not exactly innocent. The thoughts of Men+women activities had begun creeping into our young minds; as a matter of fact, some of us had begun

experimenting in those areas. So, it was a bit weird to have a young woman, full of form, beautiful and endearing simply as a partner. It was even crazy that she would make such a proposal, nonchalantly without thinking of any possibility of overtures. She had the simplest mind I had ever seen, full of purity. As much as I felt shy, I could not say NO! Her eyes beckoned on me and I got twisted beneath her gaze. I was fixed and I knew somehow that our partnership would exceed music and grow into intimacy. Did it? Yes!

I and Zara shared something unusual. We had a deep uncommon connection. We were not the regular high school couple, ours was a bit transcendental. It seemed as though destiny brought us together, to conquer territories. Our connection was such that people admired it. Everyone knew our pair and they loved us. She was also a fantastic singer and we did songs together, going from one fellowship to the other.

Truly... Some relationships are simply
beautiful pieces... A moment of our lives
that may not be in our forever.
We got into Uni the same year, had the same
years of delay and still got out the same
year. Such events are not just coincidences.
Something was happening with us; this
thing was to be our destination but you
know what they say, it takes two to Tango.
The tango dance cannot be done solo. I
believed in us, I knew we were destined to
be one forever but unfortunately, Zara did
not share the same view. She was in a faster
lane.
When we got into Uni, we continued our
beautiful relationship, attending fellowships
together, maintaining a closeness that soon
became popular and people made reference
to us from time to time. Everything was fine
with me and Zara, till she drifted into the
arms of a Man! Zara always told me she was
attracted to men way older than her. She
always let out those thoughts but somehow,
I nursed my emotions and held them back,

hoping she would see how I felt about her and give me a chance to prove that being with someone within her age range wasn't that bad after all. We were not even exactly age mates, I am three years older. So, I still do not get why I was not good enough.

Peter was the guy. She fell into his arms and gave up herself to him. She stopped hanging around me, stopped seeing me and it seemed like she was embarrassed about us. I could not bear being sent back to the battleground where I am forced to fight for my esteem; so, I moved on. Besides, there was no way on earth I could compete against such a man. He was more grown-up and better at keeping a woman. I simply did not stand a chance. As much as seeing her in school with him hurt me badly, I still moved on. I tried to find my joy by doing other things. I became more engrossed in spiritual affairs and tried to build a stronger bond with God.

Did she come back? Yes! Like a stray sheep, she made her way back. After having been subjected to unnecessary pain and depression Zara found her way back into my arms. She seemed to be different; more committed to us but slightly tougher. That innocence was gone! She was a lot more womanly. I, on my part, was a bit unfriendly too because I had not gained enough maturity to know how not to judge other people for their deeds. I was a bit too harsh towards her past decisions and often judged her. For this singular purpose, we had fallouts often. We quarreled, she called me mean, insensitive and judgmental. She began slipping away again, gradually. Till she was gone like the wind.

Our connection became severed. She would not let me in on her struggles and she was not available when I needed her the most. Zara moved on and left me again. I was not sure how to feel but I still kept holding hope. I kinda felt that one day, the destiny that brought us together will get her back to me

and make her see we are meant for each
other, and I was also working on me being a
better person for her; more accommodating
and fewer judgments.

Relationships get easier when intentions are
made bare! Building on assumptions can
wreck a beautiful piece
Fast forward to six years later, Zara is
happily married to a man in the age category
she always wanted with two kids and I am
not that man. I was hurt. I was battered. I
could not believe that all the dreams of a
happily ever after with my best friend were
void or the fact that many people who were
inspired by our bond and found a friendship
like ours are now treading on the forever
path and I am here being the abandoned
groom, being mocked by some of our friends
who thought so highly of us.

Mmmhmm.... Life and its painful throws,
just hit you right at the most unlikely spot in
the most unexpected way. You know what

was so depressing, I talked with Zara some months ago and it was crazy to find out that all these years, while I shut myself away from the world, trying to heal from the heartbreak I felt, Zara who was the principal cause did not feel she hurt me. She claimed to be utterly oblivious of my feelings for her, even after I mentioned it once or twice, even after I showed her all that care, even after I brought her close to my family and we shared letters, expressing what we felt for each other. She still claims she had no clue. She said that she knew I loved her and she loved me too but she thought our relationship was just that pure kind of love that just remained untouched, unchanged but very strong. My eyes widened with shock. C'mon, I didn't even know such a thing existed. Now, how can I bear a grudge against someone with such a view? Maybe the fault was not just hers, it was mine too. I should have been more explicit with my expressions. Well, now I know better. The next time I find another Zara, I will say

everything I feel, without holding words
back. Defining relationships saves us from
so much pain and rejection. I am gradually
letting go of the pain now. Talking with Zara
changed so much for me. There used to be a
form of tension around me, now, I see it
easing off, bit by bit. I still love her deeply.
But she belongs to someone else now and
she is happy where she is. All I have left are
memories which I will certainly hold on to
FOREVER.

DUBBY

Chapter five

A beautiful love tale

"Every year for the last ten years, me and my wife have done a reenactment of our first date.

We originally met on MySpace ;my wife had just moved to Sherman, Texas and was looking for new potential friends in the area. When she came across my profile, she added me and I accepted. After looking at her page, I noticed she was a former collegiate athlete, just like myself, and I decided to send her a message.

We played the pen pal game for a while until finally, I gathered up the nerve to ask her to lunch. We decided to meet at a Chili's restaurant close to where she was living at the time. We ended up eating and talking for four hours and the rest, as they say, is history.

Now every year, on the anniversary of our first date, I drop her off at the front of the same restaurant and she goes inside to get us a table- just like she did the night we had our first meeting. We attempt to sit in that same booth and even wear the exact same clothes we wore on our first date. The only difference over the years has been our growing family in tow.

Now we have four children, and what was once just a table for two is now a table for six."

Originally Posted by ©McSolomon on linkedin with couple's permission.

****

End Note

Your love life is only a function of the efforts the two of you make. If two do not agree, it will be strained. Beautiful love stories start with a concrete agreement between two people and a willingness to keep to this agreement; the couple in our last story for this series have proven this.

As much as there are a lot of unhappy endings out there, we cannot stop believing in Love. Love is real, it does happen. Love changes everything. We cannot lose hope entirely. We just need to believe that when the time is right, we will certainly meet our perfect match and have the fairytale we always wanted. While you wait, build on yourself. Find satisfaction in your visions and your dreams. Become a better version of yourself. True Love begins with self love. If self love is not in place, then the Love language will not be understood.